The All About Series
All About ... Canadian Animals

Canada

Red Foxes

Barb McDermott and Gail McKeown
Reidmore Books

Reidmore Books Inc.

For more information contact
Nelson Thomson Learning,
1120 Birchmount Road,
Scarborough, Ontario,
M1K 5G4.
Or you can visit our
internet site at
http://www.nelson.com

Printed and bound in Canada
3 4 5   03 02 01

Canadian Cataloguing in Publication Data
McDermott, Barb.
All about Canadian animals : red foxes

(All about series)
Includes index.
ISBN 1-896132-11-1

1. Red fox--Canada--Juvenile literature. I. McKeown, Gail. II. Title. III. Series:
McDermott, Barb. All about series.
QL737.C22M326 1998   j599.775'0971   C98-910183-5

About the Authors
Barb McDermott and Gail McKeown are highly experienced kindergarten teachers living in Ontario. Both hold Bachelor of Arts and Bachelor of Education degrees, Early Childhood diplomas, specialist certificates in Primary Education, and have completed qualification courses in Special Education. As well, Gail has a specialist certificate in Reading and Visual Arts, and Barb has one in Guidance.

Credits
Editorial: Leah-Ann Lymer, Scott Woodley
Illustration, design and layout: Bruno Enderlin, David Strand

Photo Credits
Entries are by page number.
Abbreviations: VU=Visuals Unlimited
Cover and stamp photo: Rick Baetsen
Page
1 VU/Joe McDonald
3 VU/Joe McDonald
5 Kenneth L. Asher
7 VU/Joe McDonald
9 VU/Will Troyer
11 VU/Joe McDonald
13 VU/Joe McDonald
15 VU/Will Troyer
17 VU/Will Troyer
19 VU/Ken Lucas
21 VU/Ron Spomer
23 VU/Daphne Kinzler
25 VU/Francis and Donna Caldwell
27 Kenneth L. Asher

We have made every effort to identify and credit the sources of all photographs, illustrations, and information used in this book. Reidmore Books appreciates any further information or corrections; acknowledgment will be given in subsequent editions.

Table of Contents

(All about what's in the book)

Appearance
(All about what red foxes look like)

Red foxes are **mammals** of the **deciduous** forests.

Red foxes belong to the dog family.

Red foxes can live 12 years.

Red foxes can reach 1 m in length.

Red foxes weigh 6 kg.

Red foxes have big, pointy ears.

A Red Fox

Appearance
(All about what red foxes look like)

Red foxes have 2 long, soft fur coats.

Red foxes are red or brown.

Red foxes have black fur on their legs, feet, and ears.

Red foxes have long, bushy tails.

Red foxes look like they are wearing socks.

Red foxes have 4 toes and 1 thumb on each front foot.

Red foxes have 4 toes on each back foot.

Red foxes have long, sharp, **curved claws**.

Red Foxes Have Red, Black, and White Fur

Habitat
(All about where red foxes live)

Red foxes live near forests, farms, and the shores of lakes.

Red foxes live in a **den** or a wood pile.

Red foxes have 2 **entrances** to their den.

Red foxes use their den year after year.

Red Foxes

A Red Fox Coming Out of Its Den

Habitat
(All about where red foxes live)

Red foxes use their claws to dig their dens.

Red foxes use grass and leaves to make their dens warm.

Red foxes are **nocturnal.**

A Red Fox Digging with Its Claws

Diet
(All about what red foxes eat)

Red foxes are **carnivores.**

Red foxes eat rabbits, muskrats, birds, mice, insects, fish, frogs, earthworms, snails, and eggs.

Red foxes will eat berries, seeds, and apples only if food is **scarce.**

A Red Fox with a Salmon

Diet
(All about what red foxes eat)

Red foxes hunt alone.

Red foxes have a hunting area of 3 to 8 km.

Red foxes **pounce** on their **prey** like a cat.

Red foxes use their claws to bury their food and dig out **rodents** to eat.

Red foxes bury their food in their dens and come back for it later.

A Red Fox Running for Its Prey

Predators
(All about the enemies of red foxes)

Red foxes have many enemies.

These enemies are bears, coyotes, lynxes, dogs, hawks, and eagles.

Red foxes run from their enemies and hide in their dens.

People can be enemies of red foxes, too.

A Lynx

Offspring
(All about red fox babies)

Red fox babies are called cubs.

Red fox males are called dogs.

Red fox females are called vixens.

Red fox cubs are born with their eyes closed.

Their eyes open when they are 9 days old.

Two Red Fox Cubs

Offspring
(All about red fox babies)

Red foxes have 2 to 8 babies in the spring.

Red foxes have 1 **litter** every year.

Cubs eat food that their mother has half eaten.

Cubs drink milk from their mother.

Cubs are deaf for the first 10 days after they are born.

Canada

A Mother Washing Her Cub

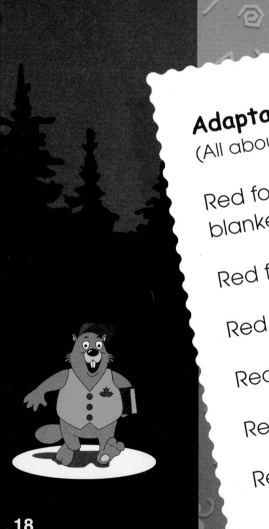

Adaptation
(All about how red foxes live in their world)

Red foxes wrap their tails around themselves like a blanket to keep warm.

Red foxes are shy and stay far away from their enemies.

Red foxes are good runners.

Red foxes can run 10 km in 1 hour.

Red foxes hold their tail straight back when running.

Red foxes put their tail down when walking.

A Sleeping Cub

19

Adaptation
(All about how red foxes live in their world)

Red foxes have good eyesight.

Red foxes have an excellent sense of smell.

Red foxes have excellent hearing.

Red foxes can hear a mouse squeaking 30 m away.

Red Foxes Have Good Eyesight, Hearing, and Sense of Smell

Special Characteristics
(All about what makes red foxes interesting)

Red foxes are good hunters.

Red foxes have 42 teeth.

Red foxes have sharp **canine teeth** for tearing meat.

Red foxes help farmers by killing mice, rabbits, and rats that eat their **crops.**

A Red Fox Ready to Hunt

Special Characteristics
(All about what makes red foxes interesting)

Red foxes have hard front teeth.

Red foxes grow a new layer of tooth **enamel** every year.

The number of layers of enamel tells the age of the red fox.

Red foxes bark and howl like dogs.

Red Foxes Have 42 Teeth

Summary
(All about the ending)

Red foxes have big ears and long, bushy tails.

Red foxes are carnivores and are good hunters.

Red foxes are truly amazing animals ... that live in Canada!

Red Foxes Barking

Glossary
(All about what the words mean)

canine teeth (page 22)
Canine teeth are sharp teeth like a dog would have.

carnivores (page 8)
Carnivores are animals who eat meat.

claws (page 2)
Claws are sharp nails on the feet of animals.

crops (page 22)
Crops are plants used for food.

curved (page 2)
Curved means rounded.

deciduous (page 1)
Deciduous refers to trees that lose their leaves
every year.

den (page 4)
A den is a place where a wild animal lives.

enamel (page 24)
Enamel is the smooth, hard, shiny, outer layer of teeth.

entrances (page 4)
Entrances are openings.

litter (page 16)
A litter is babies born at the same time from the
same mother.

mammals (page 1)
Mammals are animals who feed their babies milk.

nocturnal (page 6)
Nocturnal means active during the night instead of
during the day.

pounce (page 10)
To pounce is to jump suddenly on top of something.

prey (page 10)
Prey is an animal hunted for food.

rodents (page 10)
Rodents are a group of animals who have sharp front
teeth used for wearing away things.

scarce (page 8)
Scarce means to be in short supply.